I0138752

DRIVING
THE BEAST

SEWANEE POETRY

Wyatt Prunty and Leigh Anne Couch, Series Editors

DRIVING THE
BEAST

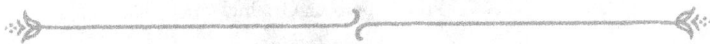

POEMS

CHRISTOPHER BAKKEN

LOUISIANA STATE UNIVERSITY PRESS
BATON ROUGE

Published by Louisiana State University Press
lsupress.org

Copyright © 2026 by Christopher Bakken
All rights reserved. Except in the case of brief quotations used in articles or reviews,
no part of this publication may be reproduced or transmitted in any format or by any means
without written permission of Louisiana State University Press.

LSU Press Paperback Original

DESIGNER: Emily A. Olson
TYPEFACE: Garamond Premier Pro

COVER PHOTOGRAPH: Unsplash/Oscar Keys

LIBRARY OF CONGRESS CATALOGING-IN-PUBLICATION DATA

Names: Bakken, Christopher, 1967–, author.
Title: Driving the beast: poems / Christopher Bakken.
Other titles: Driving the beast (Compilation)
Description: Baton Rouge: Louisiana State University Press, 2026. | Series: Sewanee poetry
Identifiers: LCCN 2025018561 (print) | LCCN 2025018562 (ebook) | ISBN 978-0-8071-
    8475-2 (paperback) | ISBN 978-0-8071-8541-4 (epub) | ISBN 978-0-8071-8542-1 (pdf)
Subjects: LCGFT: Poetry
Classification: LCC PS3602.A59 D75 2026 (print) | LCC PS3602.A59 (ebook) | DDC
    811/.6—dc23/eng/20250626
LC record available at https://lccn.loc.gov/2025018561
LC ebook record available at https://lccn.loc.gov/2025018562

. . . as you go out of the temple there is a mirror fitted into the wall.
If anyone looks into this mirror, he will see himself very dimly indeed
or not at all, but the actual images of the gods and
the throne can be seen quite clearly

—PAUSANIAS 8:37.7

CONTENTS

DRIVING
THE BEAST

INVOCATION

Sing in me a dithyramb to salt,
epics of cardamom and sage.

Cypress trees, grow taller please.
Snails, commence your racing.

Let us stoke delicious bonfires
and jig unbridled every night

on the opium sands of Dahab.
Let the cats of Sinai have their fish.

May scorpions find their blue shadows.
May the owls of blasphemy roost.

Hymn for the pelvis, hymn for the brow.
Hymn for the nobility of bread.

Loose, royal parrots from your cages.
Loose, weeping peacocks to the trees.

Sing in me of tomorrow's flung doors.
Sing as we depart small houses at last.

DRIVING THE BEAST

In the thick brush
they spend the hottest part of the day,
soaking their hooves
in the trickle of mountain water
the ravine hoards
on behalf of the oleander.
You slung your gun
across your back in order to heave
a huge gray stone
over the edge, so it rolled, then leaped
and crashed below.
This is what it took to break the shade,
to drive the beast,
not to mention a thrumming of wings
into the sky,
a wild confetti of frantic grouse,
but we had slugs,
not shot, and weren't after their small meat
but the huge ram's,
whose rack you'd seen last spring, and whose stench
now parted air,
that scat-caked, rut-ripe perfume of beast.
Watch now, he runs,
you said, launching another boulder,
then out it sprang
through a gap in some pine, brown and black
with spiraled horns,
impossibly agile for its size.
But, yes, he fell
with one shot, already an idea
of meat for fire
by the time we'd scrambled through the scree.
And that was all.
No, you were careful, even tender,

with the knife-work,
slitting the body wide with one stroke
then with your hands
lifting entire the miraculous
liver and heart,
emptying the beast on the mountain.
Later, it rained,
knocking dust off the patio stones.
Small frogs returned
from abroad to sing in the stream beds.
We sat and drank.
The beast talked to its rope in the tree.
At last you spoke:
no more, you said, *enough with mourning,*
then rose to turn
our guts, already searing on the fire.

OWL THEOLOGY

I sat alone with the god, looking up:
blank shape through an aperture of branches.
The morning wide with questions.

Who painted the leaves of the orange tree green,
left so much work unsigned, if barely framed
by the horizon's embracing wings?
Who offered me this bundle of bones?

My bones, said the god. My god, said the bones.
On and on like that for many hours
of pure confusion. Too holy for song.
Steady on a dead limb, listening.

Knowledge, better taken in pieces:
talon-cleaved, then prised to ribbons slowly.
On past the ribs to the jeweled interior.

HIVE THEOLOGY

Not water, so much as bloomed-over slime
to be gashed with a chucked stick.
The algae there was thick as evil jam.
Then, on a low bough, a house to bring down.

For an hour I lobbed the hive with stones,
speared it twice to poke out eyes
till a beard of wasps swelled from its cheeks.
I even ran up and spat at it, twice.

If you wanted to know such greatness now
you'd have to take my meanness too. It was vast.

Fools like me were easy enough to find
if you needed someone to detest
beyond your father or the church.

Runoff from the slaughterhouse would seep
down here where cows used to graze, soured
this stagnant pit to a useless mirror.

It's hard to drown on purpose in a pond,
Richard Pertzborn said, and he might know.
The wasps led me there anyway, intent
on testing the sting of my madness.

I had a spite reserved for me, by me,
a bloody urge that welled behind my eyes,
that made me slam my torso into walls,
and drove me to woods to roil a swarm.

So I taunted those gods, begged the sludge
to take me in: all of my sick, sick blood,

and the terrified freight of my body,
anything in me worthy of mud.
Oh, to be open to hurt like that.

SUNDAY MORNING

It's better, now, to state the obvious:
we sprawled in that rented bed all morning,
stunned by what we'd done to one another.

Of course we were beautiful to look at,
streaked with sweat like just-galloped horses
and still atwitch, though only then unsaddled.

Rumors of our excess should be believed.
Fellow citizens, we voted with our tongues.
When the President called, we let it ring.

Bad hankerings and our mad circus music.
Benedictions at the altar of Tom Waits.
Our diet of foie gras and heavy cream.

It's true we offered meat to foreign dogs.
When barbarian hordes rode in on mules,
we didn't bother to lock the front gate.

In fact, we'd both agreed, the night before,
not to bathe, nor cease in our debasement,
until this place knew we were here to stay.

WHITE ZINFANDEL

Again last night I dreamed the dream called Waiter.
Not the one where I arrive to give a poetry reading
but have forgotten to bring any books, so am told
just improvise (*we have a patient audience tonight*),
or in more hellish versions, *improvise while accompanied
by a harp.* No—in the dream called Waiter, I am
the only waiter, and thus the only chump in khaki pants
and a sea-blue polo emblazoned with a schooner.

The restaurant quickly fills with people whose thirst
for white zinfandel can never be sated, not even by death.
In the dream called Waiter (I should have mentioned)
it is forever 1988, and Table 11 is calling for more bread.
Table 11 wants to order. Table 11 wants another little cup
of that delicious drawn butter. And when I come to Table 11,
a smudged napkin wilting on my forearm, and finally land
their overcooked steaks, they move like a pack of feral dogs
circling a freshly shampooed dachshund and a kitten.

But in the dream called Waiter, I neglect the other tables,
whose numbers begin at one, and stretch beyond eleven,
at least as far as Milwaukee—do you see how hungry they are?
—so many we will run out of white zinfandel soon.
The hostess is nervous at her nautical pulpit: a tarnished copper
binnacle (a word the dream remembers) and ship's compass.

Hot plates are piling up on the line, but first I must fetch
ranch dressing from the walk-in cooler (Table 11), and the journey
through the kitchen is very long, the really dreamy part
of the dream called Waiter, since back there in the Dionysian
crannies of the restaurant's brain, beautiful waitresses
are snorting cocaine off the corners of patrons' credit cards,
and the kid who washes dishes is slurping up the scallops
Table 11 sent back (*but more white zin please*),

and the manager is giving all the chefs raises (just joking),
since he heard two of them dropped acid before peeling shrimp
this afternoon—and have you ever peeled shrimp on acid?
Now that's a job as fascinating as fascinating gets—but I am
a waiter in the dream called Waiter, the only one, and instead
of peeling shrimp or getting ranch, I go outside with Jake
to help with the garbage, which means to smoke weed from a carrot
he carved for that purpose, and then I am striding away
from the restaurant completely, past the apartment buildings
stacked up like plates up along the lake, and looking for my car,
which I parked somewhere around here, when Ashley
the aerobics teacher walks up, who I have wanted to kiss
(apparently) since 1988, and who is suddenly willing,
and like so many dream-kisses it is both delicious
and disconcerting, never quite over, just trailing off
in some slobbery way, like Ashley, who has suddenly fled,
but at least now I am able to fly, wheeling above the cul-de-sacs
in ways that feel quite natural, just the merest paddling,
sailing the warm currents above Middleton, Wisconsin,
with its cut grass and lake algae smells, and spying
—thanks to all the flying—my lost car (a '67 Pontiac Star Chief
with a license plate that reads YUMMY), and getting in,
and wondering where I left my keys, which means in the dream
called Waiter, remembering I am a waiter, remembering
Table 11 and their implacable thirst, not to mention all those
lozenges of broiled cod and pucks of meat waiting for me—
some poor guy with an empty briefcase, going everywhere
and nowhere in this dream and the other dream called Poetry,
knowing the ship's wheel never actually spins on its nail
above the top shelf of the bar, and as in some restaurants
and in most dreams, the compass at the door is only decorative.

LAST FEAST

On the morning of my execution,
I shaved, put on a clean shirt, and waited,
repeating to myself: *lullaby, lullaby.*

You called at daybreak to tell me
girls were sweeping ashes from the courtyard
and a fat man hung a rope on a beam.

As always, I nodded off while you spoke,
your voice a cottony valium-blue
into which my thoughts dissolved.

They granted my final wish:
a glass of rough wine
and three red fish fried in olive oil.

So I feasted in sleep, but awoke
at the edge of a wide, shallow lake.
You were standing far away, on the other side,
threading hooks and lead weights to a long line.
You wore the white dress they buried you in.

My mouth was moving, as if to speak,
saying: *save me, save me.*
But you heard, in echo, only: *beautiful, beautiful.*
In the end, that was right.

Years later, when they came for me,
they found only my empty glass and plate,
those bones sucked clean.

GOAT THEOLOGY

Those who deny everything, yet want,
hear me: always higher, out of sight,
are sweeter leaves,
and a steep plot of clover only I know.

Let there be nothing unwelcome to the tongue.
Unbind the tongue from its word and swallow.

To chew without ceasing,
even musk-thistle and thorn,
remembering the mountain's capricious grass,
gnawing the root and rind.

To mount a tree's voluptuous bark
and smear it with beard,
and mark it with funk, then ravage
a whole hillside down to its best ideas.

Not only asphodel and sedge, but rubbish and rot,
the rank ends and inedible beginnings.

Lord Azazel, goad open every throat.
I cast myself out beyond the last fence:
here at the end of all refusal.

DRUNK

When William Blake came fashionably late
to parties he'd blame it on archangels,
prophecies broadcast between the leaves
of ordinary trees in the orchard:
those who restrain desire do so because
theirs is weak enough to be restrained . . .
As in Martinsville, Wisconsin, when we
allowed Mike Meinholz to get in the car,
surely a mistake, since the wheels would start
churning up the twelve-packs of Budweiser
he never restrained himself from drinking.
We all have our excuses for wanting
to avoid conversation with mortals,
to restrain ourselves from the fools we are
in the neon light that only darkens
with beer, fears we can never quite drown.
One hundred people trapped in one small town
with just one bar, one church, and one butcher.
Expect poison from standing water,
bewildering Blake would probably say,
if he'd been around to help drag the drunk
from my Impala, down our steep driveway,
to the back lawn where he would sleep, where we
stood that night without the assistance
of good sense, grass, or Romantic verse,
and heard, I swear, a voice come from below
where the woods dropped into the gulley:
a woman in pain, we thought at first,
which nearly made us run the other way,
but then it shrieked like a snared rabbit,
or just some keening itch branches scratched,
or nothing but a dull thud in the chest,
nothing but what we wanted it to be, then,

some housecat that couldn't find its way down,
some worried awe that barely held us up,
some trembling thing in a tree we couldn't see.

THEOLOGY OF FLIGHT

Morning wind speaks a dialect of smoke,
brings news from yesterday and tomorrow:
what's burning there will soon enough burn here.

One bullet. Even a rumor of bullet
restless in the chamber of a neighbor's gun.
To run, before he arrives with his god.

Gather only what can be carried.
No litany for the uncompassed,
beyond the song of our shed weight.

How easy, then, to mistake us for a crowd
of ibis, some endangered birds, casting
thin, anonymous shadows

across the now-deserted flyways.
Rather than soar, driven by seasons,
we drift the shifting borders, anywhere,

which lead down always to a scrap
of coast, and the chained islands
of So Close, Almost There, and Too Far.

THE CROSSING

1. Lesvos

Fishermen out before dawn. None returned.
        I asked you why they left their nets behind,

but you were looking out, across to Assos,
        and maybe didn't hear me in the wind.

We both wore the same ironic mask:
        one blue eye floating upon a white sea.

On that balcony, beside the iron table,
        a geranium held on for dear life.

All day we watched waves capsize in the rain.
        Our shoreline here: the other shoreline's mirror.

Those aren't nets, you said after a long time,
        but mounds of sodden jackets and lost oars.

Stray cats sheltered in the light of the café.
        We didn't know the others huddled there.

The wind changed course and tried to explain
        by shaking the geranium, but words sank

in the crossing, so we heard under water.
        When I opened my hands, my palms burned,

as if they'd been lashed by splintered wood.
        In sleep, you told me, we have been rowing.

Truth is, no one here knows where we're going.
        I begged you not to leave, but you'd already

slung an orange scarf over your wet head.
        There aren't enough boats to carry them,

I shouted, so there's nothing left to do.
        There is, you said. I'm going down to see.

2. Assos

They would rise, the islands, enormous beasts
somehow moving faster than our ship.

They hid their faces from us, but their backs,
covered in a coarse fur of thornbushes
and clots of purpling thyme, would seem
to heave as they swam, pull us to their shores.

These were not the Ithakas we wanted,
yet each morning we docked for a while,
if we found a harbor, so some of us
could be discarded. We watched ourselves dissolve
to distance in the ship's arrowing wake,
lines of us trudging up island spines
in search of water or sheltering caves.

So we grew lighter, every day riding
higher on the waves. And we had more time.

In the galley, we feasted on our grief.
We'd spent all our lives by then, had nothing
left to decide, beyond which one of us,
last hero bound for home, would steer the empty ship.

A THRIFT STORE LANDSCAPE

unstoried, artless, unenhanced . . .

Nothing can fully ripen here,
since time stood still the moment it was made.
See how the cypresses refuse to bow,
how even the absurd, tidy wheat sheaves
assert their claims on this eternity?

Light, cast from a doubtful, unseen star
over the horizon's wobbly line
will neither brighten nor suddenly dim,
causing the poor misshapen animals
(blue cattle and what could be a donkey)
to ooze their purple shadows forever.

Festering below, in grass they'll never taste,
are the scribbled ruins of some poppies.

It's fortunate the painter lacked the skill
to render flesh—no badly made farmer
ever appears, so the three olive trees
must prune themselves, and fields remain unplowed.

Better to close your eyes than stare too long
at the distorted and meaningless
hunk of mountain—it's neither Alpine
nor Appalachian, and no one will ever
try to scale it. Who could survive
in a landscape so devoid of perspective?

This is not Greece, nor Germany, nor France.
In fact, no country's fixed a border here
because it can't exist. The soil itself
is wrong, the crops confused, the regions mixed.

Though only a minor decoration,
the smudge of crow seems right, perched upon
a detail you might easily overlook:
—it's only an angled ocher slash,
but the wooden fencepost knows why it's there:
to remember it was once a tree,
to be sturdy and hold still for the grapes,
those optimistic envoys of late summer
clustered so deep in their leafy shade
they're barely visible to the man
who comes to buy the painting over lunch.

He's just walked twelve blocks, alone in the rain.
In fact, he traveled years to get here, holding
papers from a place you don't recognize,
on boats you wouldn't recognize as boats.
His presence here is not entirely legal,
but this is only a thrift store, so no one cares.

He understands the fencepost and the grapes,
knows duty and possibility blur
in such a hopeful, unfinished place.

The mountain's big, but easily toppled.
There's nothing awful hidden in the ditch.
The animals can't eat, nor will they run.

ON THE WAY TO PANORMO

As for the impossibility of being here,
I think of the old man limping ahead of me
in the village today, a huge bag of lemons in one hand,
an olive-wood cane in the other, black wool
sweater thin at the elbows, how he stopped
once, then again, to look over his shoulder,
as if hoping to remember why, moments ago,
he dressed and left his balcony with the belief
they were—these heavy lemons—something he needed,
saying open your eyes, saying so much is already
behind you, cured inside its rind, and yet
leave anyway, it is already February, and know
the almond trees have opened their wounds to the sun,
each blossom an awareness specked with blood.

WHITETAIL THEOLOGY

In late October, early in the rut,
I'd heave up to the higher branches
and wedge myself between two wings of oak,
then grip my bow, try hard to stay still.
Nothing made that easy. Neither the cold,
nor the stampede of raw desires
that threatened to trample my boredom.
What made it worse were the ghosts
who'd hunted here before—the family line,
generations who stalked these woods,
its granite pinnacle, looking for deer.
How little I cared about shooting them.

Well before dusk my father would leave
to stomp a three-mile arc behind the wind,
forgetting his damaged hip—and for now
even the brown bottles of pills he racked
like ammunition in the black lunch pail
he hid beneath a blanket in his car.
Instead, he'd steer the deer from their grass
along the muddy banks of Blue Mounds Creek,
then run them up through scrub to where I sat.

The shame he carried: I could not forgive.
And yet, after those hard hours of hiking,
when he'd find doe, or even a spike buck
pulling clover right under my tree,
and I wasn't asleep, but reading a book,
he'd say nothing. We were not eloquent
like that, not with our disappointments.
The deer would raise tail and run. We'd drive home.

As the Greek myths go, there are few good fathers.
Sons are abandoned on barren hillsides,

left to starve. Others are simply devoured,
gore for the monsters who engendered them.
And Zeus: a flagrant serial sadist.
At best, men are titans for a few hours,
small gods who stride beside the ancestors
to lift us, while they can, from chariots
into bed, setting all our weapons aside.
And though he must have held him in his arms
(that boy who lost his wings, the boy who fell)
not even poor Daedalus could save his son.
No wonder I could not save my father.

ANIMAL SONG

The way the barn's angled, shingled roof shoulders off the light
may be the proof I need—though of what, I don't really know.

Night had its fill, but morning arrived famished, ready
to feast. I woke remembering that I am brutal,

a penned beast. No dream weight, the mind's reviving mass.
More like a crumbling fence held up by whips of berry thorn.

But I can see my breath, red clouds, trees. Doubt, an open field.
Inside, the cow and a few horses clamor for their hay.

FOR THE DEAD UNION

a savage servility slides by on grease

After summer rain, the old-growth forest
behind Greendale Cemetery fills
with eerie promise—boletes, milk-caps,
and terraces of pink-white oysters,

while the veterans of remembered wars
doze on beneath deep mattresses of moss
and gaudy rhododendrons wide as mansions.
Even this far west, five hundred miles

from Bunker Hill, Daughters of the Revolution
have graves to tend, as do the offspring
of those who fell at Shiloh and Khe Sanh.
Fresher mud roofs the new pandemic dead.

Paying no heed to local history,
remote or absurdly new, quick streams gush
the layered shale embankments, cut ravines
so steep old gravestones sometimes slide

from their tidy, metered plots to murmur
obituary greetings from below.
I often brush their faces clear of dirt
while out foraging, sounding out the names.

If the rains are right, by mid-July
the first chanterelles tunnel up through leaves,
timid as small flames for a day, before
rising bold as Corinthian columns

into the mist—fluted, comically orange,
and not reeking of funeral soil

but scented improbable apricot,
hints of death's most subtle literacy.

≈

Atop the city's other distinguished hill,
the college buildings shrug, clutch their ivy.
The old observatory, named for Captain Newton,
who fought with the Union at Corinth,

is really just another church—its design
cruciform, compassed north, domed with green copper,
its Doric narthex cheerful as a crypt.
The students stroll downhill only for booze,

wary of the red-capped, red-faced whites
who fly the Dixie flag from their new trucks
and shop at Giant Eagle packing heat,
the same men who join militias in the woods

across French Creek, where young George Washington
once paddled his canoe. On Braveheart Radio
the new patriots whine and stockpile ammo,
their sniggers ringing in the city's ears.

Some years back, I read a student essay
that not once, but twice referred to Lowell's
"For the Dead Union" by mistake, a bit
too apt, only months after Charlottesville.

My children practice active-shooter drills
at school, though I fear almost as much in-
active shooters, my well-armed small-town
neighbors, who see mostly through the dark glass

of their rage. Tonight, carting groceries to my car,
I had to dodge a pickup flying an upside
down American flag. On bumper rust:
BELIEVE IN GOD NOT GOV SCIENCE.

Our city boomed in the cross-hairs
of an infant nation—a halfway stop
on the New York to Chicago rail,
and a stop, too, for those running north

underground: at his busy safe house
near the corner of Liberty and Arch,
the freedman Richard Henderson
sheltered hundreds, working the secret line

a local firebrand had established
out of his tannery in New Richmond
—young John Brown, who buried his first wife
and two children on a hill behind his barn.

Downtown, at Diamond Park, the cast-iron fish
of the faux-Bernini fountain gasp,
since their water was turned off years ago.
The new, most savage servility here

bends low to the con, believing nothing
but what's been fetched from the extremes
of explanation: the virus a hoax,
and micro-chips, and deep state cabals,

with a million orange ballots hid somewhere
in a blue car with Arizona plates.

The local Klan are now just Oath Keepers,
dismissing any mention of a coup.

In my Night Owl hockey league, machinists,
plumbers, and professors hit the ice, work
off their beer. On the trophy, last season's
champs christened their team The White Nationalists.

～

A thousand small-town Midwestern greens
are now deserted as dead factories,
guarded by bronze, musket-clutching soldiers,
who can't recall which fields, of which republic,

are engraved on the plaques at their feet,
nor how many Lenape or Shawnee
were scythed to speed the frantic engines
of American pastoral. *In the woods*

we return to reason and faith . . .
until faith bends reason towards disbelief
in the great frontier towns, whose fates are geared
to the greater green lights of commerce.

Like Talon, now gone for thirty years,
where generations fed their fortunes
making zippers—patented here in 1914.
The city nearly died when the plant moved east.

I have tried to remain one of the roughs
all my life, but maybe we've had enough
of roughness now. As I marched across campus
at dusk, I scared an owl from its hollow

in a split oak by the observatory.
I thought of the telescope inside,
good for looking far away from here,
and the quiet power of such refraction,

those quick bends in the direction of light.
At the base of the owl's rotting tree,
a clump of Jack-o'-lantern mushrooms
were casting spores, just beginning to glow.

A DEFENSE OF POETRY

A harbor town empty this afternoon
    of all reason by the time
the martyred letters had arrived.

No reflections hurry past
    the papered glass of the shop window.
The heat's blare muted by no shade.

No time for oracles now:
    not even a radio will sing this late.
Blank gaze of linen pinned to a line.

A mocking ceremony of geranium.
    The stupidity of mortar and stone
against the perfect sea's monotony.

Yet there, at the end of the dock, someone
    taut with concentration, almost
immobile—a statue, maybe—is hauling

fist over fist an invisible net, heavy
    as the air soars through it, ignites
the gills of fish gasping in their pail.

THEOLOGOS

Somewhere the bushes torched, and brittle pines
cast shrapnel into the needled blanket
ten seasons had woven down Livadi,
across ridges all the way to Thimonia.

One hour to melt the water lines
a generation of men believed
could quench the valley's thirst.

The word raced towards Astrida,
consuming groves, stables, and nests,
turning ground-doves into torches,
sparing only the Archangel on the cliff.

The oldest trees unringed themselves to ash,
were hollowed into towers lit with eyes.

Rabbits, too, heard the word, then dashed
into their dying, bearing light to riverbeds
where more dusty tinder waited to speak.

Lives not smaller than ours, but greater.
To speed headlong, blow embers, and stoke,
then smolder by the furthest village walls
into cathedrals of snowy fur and bone.
The rest the word forgot, allowed to burn.

AFTER THE SIGHING

When at last you went to Vergina and saw
    the golden diadem set with lapis lazuli,

then sped to Agia Eleni on a quarter-tank
    to swelter in the hut where they prepare
their dance across a bed of living coals
    (hours of lyre and drums, the icon sighing),

you understood we invented the gods
    in the service of Beauty, and her lover, Pain.

The silence after an explosion is often
    as terrible as the explosion. The fixed eyes
of the maenad after her roaring, more than
    her awful roaring. To see an old woman's feet

crush fire, then lift, black stockings
    melting up her ankles, and not be burned.

Such faith, knowing only blindness will follow.
    After the sighing, how quiet the village was,
all of us walking away from the ashes.
    Even the dancers, now released by their saint.

To recall, only now, the long drive back:
    the bike's one headlight slicing curves.

You ran out of gas outside Provatas,
    hiked across fields to find a station,
singing and carrying stones in case of dogs,
    baffled by the blankness between stars.

The same Greek darkness swallows all travelers.
    Vergina and Agia Eleni vanishing too.

Only seconds persist: those mornings at the wood oven
    in Pylea. Hard work believing you were offered
such bread—the bronze crust shattered as it cooled.
    Or, by the Minoan tombs at Armeni:

a goat gnawing free from a tangle of thorns
    to feast on rock rose and mountain sage.

From such distance, you might begin to see
    how steady earth holds beneath each loss
(slow chisels of the stone-cutters cutting the stones).
    Don't open your eyes—some shadows

are still being fed. Kyria Athanasia
    cooked you beans and zucchini from her yard.

Olives. Cold water drawn from the stream.
    (Samothraki, or lost again in Pelion?)
And that was joy, you might say, knowing better.
    Given shape as much by pain then, as now.

Swimming out beyond the horse-shaped cape.
    A green tent. Scorched vineyards dreaming

of wine behind the empty beach.
    All along, gold and lapis lazuli at rest
in their burial mound, waiting to gleam.
    Stay with them and be polished by sand.

Or sing *evening* and *pomegranate,*
    evening and *pomegranate*—pour them out.

Find any suitable tongue. *Ligo benzini, parakalo.*
    Just enough to carry you over Hortiatis.

There are so many ways to leave.
    Don't hurry, knowing it's all about to burn.

Clutch the bone-handled knife your father gave you,
    and sleep now, not far at all from the sea.

ROTHKO THEOLOGY

Untitled (Black on Gray), 1970

In time, the sky devoured the hill,
freeing three shades of darkness from the trees.
I woke you, carried you to the window,
so we could look for what we'd failed to see.
Maybe it would move if we held still,
what we had measured with our dreaming.

As if it awaited our arrival.
As if air rattled when it shook its frame.

Our breathing slowed, but it wouldn't let us go.
When it rose and sloughed its shadow,
too slowly to tell if it moved toward us
or away, if it flew, or nested there,
at last we saw. Not less than light. Not more.
Our eyes weren't open then. Nor were they closed.

PAESTUM

That April, for instance,
to watch a storm blow in from the gulf,
cloud-front shoring ranks on the horizon,

arrowheads of swallows slicing a wind
            strong enough to set their wings on fire,

but not the weather so much as the place itself,
            how my daughter scampered up a tree
so she could comprehend the view
down-mountain to the plains of Paestum,

            how the resident sheepdog
leaped into the air to bring down lemons
from the branches he could reach.

                  That kind of desire.
That readiness for satisfaction.
To be wrung out, my sodden heart,
            by any visible thing.

How the raised arms of the vineyard
called down the atmosphere, made it ring.

Grilled artichokes on the road to Pompeii
            with the flavor of the Underworld in them.

The rain, astonished into four minutes of hail.

                  And Etruscan honey.
And my small son's wish to be a conquering god,
            which he dared speak aloud.

No matter. The Temple of Poseidon was busy
casting long, indifferent shadows.

The whole re-invaded town so ruined
by its ancient hangover,
even the wine spoke with a Greek accent there.

MONOLITHOS

In memoriam, Jack Gilbert and Linda Gregg

We ask about the poets who lived in a shack
by a well that went dry decades ago, but no one
remembers them. Now, just two widows
and a calico cat, a green truck embroiled in cactus,
and the café in the main square, closed:
all present as facts, guarding their silence.
Like dutiful new recruits, black beetles
march across the volcano's barren face
while scorpions hoard their poison
behind the crude slats of an old toolshed.
A few white walls square their shoulders still,
but the wooden gates have divorced their hinges.
What do they know of the woman and man
who raised their own walls here
across a few miraculous seasons? No one
remembers what they said or cooked
or if they spent days naked in the yard,
shameless as they darkened for midsummer.
No one remembers, yet it's easy to see
what is sacred here—not one stone, but a thousand
strewn singularities, blown free of us,
like the boy we passed as we were leaving,
who leaped from his Minoan fresco
this decade or some other century
to rush past us with his haul of fish,
bound for what was left of Monolithos,
his skin untarnished bronze, his hair spilled ink,
his bare feet kicking cyclones of dust,
a ghost already before we were gone.

NEGATIVE THEOLOGY

Case in point: the ear's empty theater.
Or the relentless, metered heart.

The unseaworthy trireme of the brow.
Even the pelvis and its one want.

Always mounting, the evidence against us.
Case in point: the insufficient foot.

We don't know anything. Yet here, again,
the sun's perpetual choir, silent as ever.

Proof enough to keep us guessing.
Plenty to fill our sad little urns.

Reaching with all the strength I never had,
both shadows and fire drain through my fingers.

THEOLOGY AT BLACK EARTH CREEK

The creek I loved propelled itself
through soybeans, corn, and three small towns
before it tired of Dane County's
Atrazine and suburban sprawl
and stalled under a railroad bridge,
became the hole where suckers
would rise to mutilate our worms.

Reagan hadn't killed the Russians
yet, and they hadn't yet killed us.
The world was toxic and beautiful,
still safe, at least, for everyone
ignorant and Lutheran like me.
Really, I cut classes hoping
to set my own idiocy in stone.

You could follow the railroad
all the way to Mazomanie
and the creek would never be more
than half a field away, veering
along slopes the glacier riddled
into the granite. Parallel,
dull, Highway 14 ran there too.

That's where I'd park the Pontiac,
tie hooks and slather on the Off.
You had to cross a nettle-ditch
to get there, and rusty barbed wire
my uncles hadn't bothered to clip.
Trespass enough on anything
and you stake a claim upon it.

But we didn't really own the hole;
the land owned us, in its own way.

With the church bells out of earshot,
we dragged our tackle here to brood.
In town, a man named Peterson
babbled on about catching God,
said something pulled his bobber down,

snagged the line on one of the drowned
limbs at bottom. It did not rise.
He was still there in Black Earth
drinking his way back up, or down,
as he'd been taught. From what I knew,
biggest thing ever pulled from the creek
was a carp the size of a dog.

The creek babbled no rejoinder
in answer to my confessions,
just hurried every lie I spat
downstream to bother the cut grass.
I think of all the fish I killed
because I could, so terrified
I'd come to kill myself instead.

I was too weak for that. But I could
come in winter to crack the ice,
stomp windows into creek water
clearer for being cold, being here,
miles from the village where my people
believed they had been hooked on sin,
where I'd watch trout float belly up.

THEOLOGY IN NEGRIL

If I had not forgotten how to pray,
    I might have spoken, Lord of Smoke,
but I just rolled and then burned a long time
    in the lap of a breadfruit tree,
while lions came out to bathe themselves at dawn.

Late gratitude for everything I missed
    and for all that I remember.
The throb of bass and the treble of waves.
    A palm's machete shredding wind.
Old jar darkened by the prophet's honey.

You were the grackle announcing the sun.
    In sugar, in shackles, in rum.
Inside the current and also the cliff,
    you washed the cane field's open wound
and scoured the sea for unburied bones.

In everything you took, in all you gave.
    In the cleft of a split mango.
In fine sand brushed from a thigh:
    the body's perfection, once again.
Three days without clouds, then rain on the skin.

In small streams you hid, waiting for a flood.
    In the color blue's wet vowels.
In the ray, the shark, the coral, the conch.
    I never asked for your blessing.
For all the ways I didn't have to ask.

MORNING SEA

Don't make me stop. Don't make me see
the way a small fishing boat, even when stalled
on blocks for winter, reflects sun
from its dingy hull, on a morning
too bright to be trusted.

Don't make me stand. Let me deny what I see
(I didn't look long—the boat might not be real).
Let me drag my gaze from where it caught,
and run, not looking back, never
insulting what's still here.

THEOLOGY AT DALABELOS

Early this morning a starling, just arrived from Tripoli or Tangier,
      paced an hour beneath the lemon tree.
After so long away, I am startled too, finding myself here
      another March, unsettled by the pathos
of the mandarins and wild mustard, who are so in love
      with this place they give wholly of themselves,
both sweetness and heat. I thought to try again the vain labor
      of remaining in one place, remembering
the constant failure in me—restless attention, more the lack of it,
      like barely nuzzling the surface of a stream.
But I hunger, and am kneeling now in a patch of *papoules*
      (of the tribe of legume), emerald unfurlings
with leaves bent for cupping sun: at each narrow tip
      small tendrils, like early beards, for clinging
and climbing. I will take them before the root, clipping
      the stems between thumbnail and forefinger,
eat them later with strong vinegar and good oil.
      Let's grant each leaf one grain of salt.
Entries into the index of spring. Please find tomorrow, before
      it's too late, some *ladaniá,* Cretan rockrose,
and more of the wild carrot's scrimshaw tops, then *throubi,*
      down on the ridge—surly ancestor of thyme—
whose resin will still live on your hands for days.
      You'll find me climbing and clinging to a bunch
of *stamnagathi,* prince of all chicories, whose bitterness exceeds my own,
      I suspect, since I am the only being here
a little shy about the bees and almond blossoms—seeing how
      they throw themselves into longing headfirst,
are not ashamed, then hum the pollen onto their backs.
      And so, I walk, not stopping to gather sow-thistle,
to visit the oldest tress, who slump half-asleep between
      their soft stone terraces. They rarely speak,

but their bark has cured to an eccentric braille some can still read.
       Not me. Yet there, in a narrow valley of one olive's thigh,
a single poppy seed found enough earth, hid like a secret:
       is out viewing things at last, through one blind eye.

OCTOPUS THEOLOGY

To know pain, I ate my own leg.
This is a way of suffering:
I tunnel into my darkness,
a cave of ink, then become one
in a ring of unburied stones.
So I attend, God of Stillness.
Permit me my devouring.
From each stump, another leg grows.

NOTES FOR THE INVASION

A storm worked all night to flood us out
—revealed we are not innocent.

An old stone wall. A regiment of artichokes
in green and silver rows: all their weapons

ready, but not yet the awful purple flowers
whose songs are practiced somewhere underground.

Wind rifles the weary eucalyptus,
searching for papers that won't prove a thing,

and rain muffles the snapdragons' red bells.
Never mind. Ants will soon come forth

(the most relentless among us) to carry off
what little remains of a drowned moth.

If we turn away from such mirrors,
blind to what is clear, we should be made

to march, to carry the corpses ourselves;
we should eat only thistles the rest of our lives.

JANUARY SWIM

First dive of the year, lured into the cove
        by the old stone dragons of Ierissos,
who have, by January, converted the water to flame

—thinking of my friend Adam, who would float
        for hours at Chora Sfakion on Crete,
or, other summers, at the placid edge of Kos or Kardamyli.

He once wrote from Preveli, impressed
        by the *wild, muscular orthodoxy*
conveyed by the statue of a monk with a machine gun.

He sometimes settled for Sardinia,
        though he would have loved Ierissos, had he
not died last April in Krakow. He last wrote at Easter,

said he was busy scribbling poems and shaping
        something on Brodsky—that my new son
had arrived with a message: *The future exists. Don't worry.*

He loved lindens and Gregorian chant
        (in small doses, taken like a potion).
He was a poet of doubt and rapture,

always moored to earth by books, black cats,
        and the sight of his beloved wife's face.
Swimming too. And Seferis's great poem, "The King of Asini,"

inspired by a Homeric footnote.
        At Ierissos, my wife and son are pacing the sand.
We have a long drive to reach the future. I am shivering

and very tired of death (*just sadness, that's all*),
        like Seferis in 1945,
wrung out by war and distrustful of words, but suddenly moved

when a blind man in Athens made his way
        past the bullet-riddled walls and stepped right
into the fire, playing Greek anthems on his harmonica.

Adam was born that same year in Lvov,
        to a Europe of shabby anthems, sublime
blindness—with all the wounds Seferis promised. Also, the sea.

THESSALONIKI

After, when the goddess fled, we plowed her clay,
stacked temple blocks, a church.

Her ancient road has almost been disrobed.
All along it's been here, under the new road,
down about the distance of a spear.

For eighty years the same orange cat has slept
in the missing synagogue's shadow, purring in Ladino.
Now, to honor some dignitary, fighter jets strafe
the bay, shattering the city's mosaic dome.

But when you lifted the saint's rib from its pillow,
I too smelled myrrh—for a moment believed.

Hooded crows still gather to pace like monks,
and each day roosters wail for the recent dead,
while some new god gallops to war on a red horse,
whose hoofprints will remain visible in stone
there atop the highest Roman walls.

DAYS OF 1993

He'd leave the village to its dust,
hike a shepherd-trail over the ridge
and pitch his tent in a hidden inlet
where no one would see the driftwood fire.

Every day, he'd follow unmarked roads
along the coast—perfectly alone,
swimming and sobbing, splayed
with the lizards on those temples of marl.
Sometimes he'd push on for an hour, then stop
to write the same line over again
in the blank book he kept inside his pack.

Always thirst. Always wild sage.
And as many sea urchins as gods.
Juniper, ravaged by the awful sun.

There was someone he might have loved
in Vourvourou, further up the coast.
And always Cavafy, calling from Egypt.
It was over soon, that wonderful life.
Like that, he began: waterless,
wind-wrenched, cleaving to rock.

THEOLOGY AT KIONIA

I searched that underworld for signs, knowing
only what my body said was true,
the sea around me murky as light

cast through salt—not transparently there,
yet something to be savored by the mouth
my cupped hands made when I dove deeper in.

Cove where you wrecked me, Catastrophe,
I heard your voweled song from fathoms down.
You blew into my clay and I became.

When I found the kiln-hardened handle
and the fissured lip, I held and heaved,
then lurched my way back to burning air.

This amphora I dredged from your sand
might still hold water. Come, I'll fill it with wine.

REMBETIKA THEOLOGY

From the top of some distant minaret,
      the voice of the mangas dropped.
It spilled over gutters and cobblestones
then trickled west into shanties,
      where the poor knelt beside cookfires
and smoked away their ache.

A brief litany for the one, *aman,*
      aman, who rises now to dance,
stoned dervish, reeling in his secrets.
Another round and more cigarettes
      to rouse the weary baglamas
and raise the hackles of the tambourine.

The police won't bother us tonight.
      And since the hour of prayer has ended,
even the monk might swing by for a puff.
Tomorrow, one more Sunday of clouds
      to help us rehearse an anguish
we've embraced since nineteen twenty-two.

Let's fill each filthy alleyway with song.
      Nothing so holy as a dirge.

THEOLOGY ON IKARIA

The winding way up, Kampos to Pigi.
A thick stick to hack away the thorns.

Seven years. What had been hidden in earth
now rises to sing and die in the trees.

All forms are dismantled into music.
Not just the body's, but the mind's husk, too.

A peach abandons its pit on the plate.
From ordinary grapes: this ancient wine.
From the shore to the mountain, a long time,
climbing the stone path, before the roads.

Old thoughts chorus on the branches–poor things.
Some new thoughts will join them there soon.
I believe, for now, what I don't understand.

Someone came before me to place the stones.
So much labor for nothing less than me.

TURNING FIFTY AT THE ORACLE OF DEATH

Cape Taenaron, Mani

A few wrong turns brought me here to the end,
so far south the land ran out of itself,
open sea devouring all but this slab
of dusty headland inscribed by high wind.
I obeyed the ancient instructions, left

my rented car behind and went by foot
to find the cave—*the drawing place of ghosts.*
Ventilation shaft of the underworld.
Here the living came to sip at death.
Would I even know which questions to ask?

Half a century old and I was still
a ruin-addict, clomping haunted sites
in my flip-flops, hoping to rouse the mind
with a whiff of information and myth
in between long swims and cold seaside beers.

I'd never liked to predict my next move.
Yet for this cheerful destination,
I'd read a book, even opened a map.
In fact, prediction was what drew me here;
looking out for death, listening

at least, for its mute, insistent murmur,
was what I had been doing every day
since, as a boy, I learned I had to die.
When you come to the Oracle of Death,
push your head through, find a road going down

that no one travels. That same road led
into a labyrinth of storm drains
I discovered when I was ten
beneath the streets of Madison, Wisconsin.
Those crumbling tunnels were ankle-deep

with rain water and rills of fallen leaves.
I lost myself down there, and yet
emerged from a manhole five blocks from home.
I'd followed where the unlit current led.
Fifty, now: why not get lost again?

I trudged the sweltering peninsula,
but found only old walls, a broken church.
The famous cave, I learned, was further out;
you had to go by boat and then dive in.
So many years spent tunneling back

into passages I wouldn't remember:
every hour sacred, but rigged for collapse.
Burial rites we rehearse each birthday.
Which is to say there's really no way back,
and this far south, left and right are the same.

Anyway, the afternoon was dying.
The map of the Mani I'd unfolded
was still there in my car to be ignored.
The end of one continent at my feet:
nothing to do now but turn north and walk.

SONNET

Late June. A dry riverbed
lined on both sides with tall reeds.
They went quietly—away
from the beach—to find a flat
stretch of sand between some trees.
They had gone there once before.
Got what they wanted again,
then took their time gathering
smooth white stones to mark the place.
No one had seen. But when they
hurried back downstream, night had
softened the cliffs, and crickets
were already improvising
their bawdy mantinades.

GNOCCHI

For breath to enter, hands must wait,
hold nothing till the water boils.

The patience of a wooden slab.
The purpose of a heavy pot.

Then an egg, warmed up in the palm,
but no real measurement of flour

beyond what the potato wants.
After a week of snow-melt, fog,

it wants so much today. You must
guide the arrival of enough,

borrow some steam from the water,
make thickened air more than a dough.

The salt, the hand, the touch, the board.
What yields willingly and what holds:

a finger-weight rolled off the fork.
Window of butter, leaf of sage.

GORGONA

I.

Harbor shrine filled with candles and saint-stuff:
the wives of fishermen come here to pray.

Like them, you were drawn by myrrh
and the heat of a burning wick.

But that heat isn't your heat anymore.

You'd come back to view your photo
in its halo of cave and waxlight.

But that face isn't your face anymore.

You surrendered yourself to me
when your ship went down at Thimonia.

That was years ago. A distant drowning.

But you keep forgetting, and arrive
with a bunch of thyme, a sign you drop

for the living to see. It gives them hope,
though you know that is forbidden.

You crossed a line we'd set, one marked
by beehives and the whitewashed church,

but returned while I was rinsing myself
with pump water from a shattered cup.

A ring of salt had formed around my feet,
and anchors I'd collected were piled

under the mastic tree, seething with flies.
You said: *my door.* I said: *come through.*

Fall back into me now, little ghost.
Let go of the shore.

2.

We'd meet each morning at the ruins,
but I'd change shape, and then you couldn't see.

Last week: a sparrow. One day: a pile of sand.
And then I became a thing as close
as I could come to being myself:
a soft, barbed succulent sprung up for light
through a cleft in the wind-washed granite.

That summer of advances and retreats
left us exhausted, knowing such thirst.

You begged me to stay, move out of the shade,
but I'd halt at the temple's crumbling sill,
then go, leaving a stone on your tongue.

Every day you'd return with the imprint
of my scales on your thighs. You could taste me.

In the yard, a withered tree greened, then roused
one olive from a thousand willing blossoms.

Soon I stopped appearing in any form
your body understood. No, you still had this:
some mornings you'd hear me furrowing
the stillness of the lagoon with my tail.

3.

The boats are coming in, you said at last,
your back to me, your attention anchored
to what moved beyond the porthole window
above our little sink. In a tin sieve,
wild grapes you'd gathered years ago, too ripe
for anything but vinegar now.
Whole seasons leaked away like that. Here, gone.

The going out, the coming in, the waves.
Bits of severed net still clung to your wrists,
but every mirror proved us beautiful,
out of water as much as in. Learning slow,
what an island means. That single lesson,
rehearsed so many nights, by lantern light,
as you brushed broken coral from my hair.

BREAD THEOLOGY

At last, the blackened dome obeyed
and the god's clear eye expanded.

For us, great loads of oak were split.
For us, these patient hours of fire.

All we could have needed: even
the well water's additional grace.

In time, we harvested breath,
then lifted grain beyond itself.

And who rose at dawn, took kindling,
and commanded the heat to bloom?

The one now dusted with ashes,
who brings these riven tablets down.

DAYS OF 2006, '07, AND '08

He had given up trying to measure distance,
though each morning the odometer clicked

between garage and school, school and garage.
Whole months calculating triage, each day

thrashed between duties and urgencies, knowing
crisis is always first to fill its plate.

Just outside, crows would assemble for hours
before movement, like well-trained regiments,

then fly off to the next battlefield of white pine.
It's possible all he ever needed

was a wall of tall trees, and a battle to lose,
and the terms of surrender clear at last.

How far away are you, weary emergencies?
Scissors tucked in your bedsheets, and green pills

cocooned by foil in every drawer, and gold padlocks
—easily picked—on cupboards in the den.

Turns out there is no having that can't be undone.
Yet when he reverses the telescope,

points it from the giant eye of now, all he sees
is blameless, lucid, unvarnished by myth:
a branch of bay leaves just cut from the tree.

How his children, then, waded out to wait for waves,
paused motionless, like figures on a frieze,
and leaped over each break, light as dolphins.

LAST DOG

I had another dog put down today.

When I say "I," I wish I didn't mean
me, the man I am—a coward
too afflicted with hope to put down
his own selfishness long enough to do
what my father would when "today" came.
He'd shake the familiar leash by the door,
then out into the field the man and dog
would walk, but only he would return,
missing one bullet in the rifle,
an empty leash now holding nothing back.

That's right, when I say "put down," we know
what I mean. How easily we lie about that.
We "put down" an empty coffee cup.
We "put down" the phone after bad news comes.
No. The doctor was kind, his work was hard.
The family huddled with her on the floor,
the children more composed than the adults.
He had to steer through our clinging arms
to find a vein and work the small syringe.
Then we couldn't put our dog back up again.

When I say "another," I mean I've had
two dogs die in four years, an accounting
measured by black urns on a bookshelf.
The first dog grew so old she couldn't walk.
Her ashes: light as a pile of feathers.
By the time today arrived, the second
dog's brain was mostly tumor, so she walked,
but in one tight circle, like a puppy
chasing her tail too slowly, unable to stop.
Her ashes: heavy as an overflowing bowl.

When I say "dog," I mean incorrigible,
bull-headed, shit-eating, slobber-jowled
Athena, born without a sense of shame,
and far less wise than her name would suggest.
I say "dog," admitting, in overtly
sentimental terms, some days I forgot
she was a dog, so much a part of me
she had become. It might be true that all
her six short years she was in pain, the tumor
causing her to pounce on me, then press
the horse-weight of her head into my chest.
But I'm not afraid to call an embrace
what it is, even between dog and man.

                    Yes, when I say "had,"
I admit I left the work to someone else.
Still, the missing weight of "had."
Truth is, Athena was always leading me,
each evening down the sidewalks of our town,
or in the forest, which we stormed off-leash.
Again today, before the doctor came,
when she rose into her best attempt at sit,
then panted in my face, I sat up too;
for us both, one last and right rehearsal
of an agreement we'd always understood.

NOCTURNE

I rinsed my face from a garden hose,
midnight in the quiet ink of Crete,
led home by stone and faithless hands
to wait like Mandelstam

for the earth to be axed in half.
Knowing it will be. But as before
water spilled over me
back to clay, was taken up again,

and I had just spent hours, eyes
open, drenched in lute music—
helpless notes, no longer lost.
Every chorus surging.

DAYS OF 2015

Τα καλοκαίρια μας μικρά
κι ατέλειωτοι χειμώνες

We seized the night, and shook it till it broke,
so time and bottles and most of our shoes
spilled from its breaking—and music gushed too:
Paris and Nikos relentless until five.

Blame them for this minefield of broken glass,
our unreasonable outbursts of joy.
Someone danced till his knees were bleeding.
Someone said she had fractured her being.

Then that night ended. Then sun, as before.
Now the instruments unwind in their coffins,
and we pace along the balcony and stare.
The broken girl is asleep on last night's chair.

Some say we have tonight. Tomorrow too.
In the fireplace, a few embers glow.
Brother, bring me some coffee. OK, and beer.
We're going to need at least a thousand years.

ACKNOWLEDGMENTS

Thanks to the editors of the following publications, where these poems first appeared, sometimes under another title:

Academy of American Poets, *Poem-a-Day:* "Driving the Beast" and "Lesvos"; *Birmingham Poetry Review:* "Theologos," "Theology at Black Earth Creek," "Theology at Kionia," "Theology in Negril," and "Whitetail Theology"; *Blackbird:* "A Thrift Store Landscape"; *The Common:* "Theology at Dalabelos" and "Theology of Flight"; *Copper Nickel:* "Animal Song" and "Last Feast"; *Cortland Review:* "Days of 1993" and "Sunday Morning"; *Drunken Boat:* "Hive Theology"; *The Eloquent Poem* (Persea, 2019): "Assos"; *Gettysburg Review:* "Monolithos"; *Hopkins Review:* "Bread Theology" and "Turning Fifty at the Oracle of Death"; *JuxtaProse:* "Gorgona"; *Lily Poetry Review:* "A Defense of Poetry," "January Swim," and "Morning Sea"; *Literary Imagination:* "Paestum"; *Los Angeles Review:* "Invocation"; *Michigan Quarterly Review:* "Days of 2015," "Nocturne," "Rembetika Theology," and "Thessaloniki"; *Orion:* "Octopus Theology"; *Ploughshares:* "Drunk"; *Plume:* "For the Dead Union," "Goat Theology," "Last Dog," and "White Zinfandel"; *Poetry Northwest:* "Negative Theology" and "Owl Theology"; *Salamander:* "Rothko Theology"; *Sewanee Review:* "On the Way to Panormo"; *Southern Review:* "Theology on Ikaria"; *Swing:* "Gnocchi" and "Notes for the Invasion."

"Negative Theology" also appeared in *Braving the Body* (Harbor Anthologies, 2024).

"Octopus Theology" also appeared in *Unnatural Disasters* (Orion Books, 2024).

"Theology at Black Earth Creek" won the Collins Prize at the *Birmingham Poetry Review* in 2020.

Thanks to the Virginia Center for the Creative Arts, where many of these poems were written, along with the support of Allegheny College; thank you to Leigh Anne Couch, Wyatt Prunty, James Long, and the LSUP team for shepherding this book into print in the Sewanee Poetry series. Alan Michael Parker and Corey Marks offered helpful comments on this manuscript in its early stages. Warm thanks to Natalie Bakopoulos, Scott Cairns, Joanna Eleftheriou, Panayotis League, Amanda Michalopoulou, Aimee Nezhukumatathil, Dustin Parsons, Courtney Zoffness, and the rest of the Writing Workshops in Greece family for their insights and their joy. Deepest thanks and gratitude to my first reader and partner, Allison Wilkins Bakken, and to my children: Sophia, Alexander, and Theokritos.

NOTES

The book's epigraph is from Pausanias, *Description of Greece,* trans. Jones and Ormerod, 1918.

"Driving the Beast": The poem borrows a phrase from Robert Frost's "The Most of It."

"White Zinfandel": The poem's first line riffs on the opening of James Merrill's "The Mad Scene."

"Drunk": The italicized portions are from Blake's *The Marriage of Heaven and Hell.*

"Theology of Flight": "At the onset of the unrest in Syria in 2011 the fate of the last Northern Bald Ibis colony of the Middle East was sealed with only one pair left. 2015 was the first year that no bird returned to the breeding grounds in Palmyra." Gianluca Serra, *The Last Flight of the Ancient Guide of Hajj* (2017).

"The Crossing": The coastal town of Assos, Turkey, is located on the same peninsula as the city of Troy. The ramparts of Assos are crowned by the ruins of a Temple of Athena—from those ruins, the Greek island of Lesvos is visible just across a narrow strait. In the past decades, thousands of refugees fleeing war and persecution have drowned off the coast of Assos while attempting to reach Lesvos in small boats and rafts.

"A Thrift Store Landscape": The epigraph is from Robert Frost's "The Gift Outright."

"For the Dead Union": The poem borrows its epigraph and several other phrases from Robert Lowell's "For the Union Dead." Information about the Newton Observatory at Allegheny College was gathered from the Library of Congress's Historical American Buildings Survey. "In the woods we return to reason and faith" is from Emerson's "Nature."

"Theologos": In 2016, a forest fire spread over the southeast portion of the island of Thasos, threatening the inland village of Theologos and the Archangelos Monastery.

"After the Sighing": The poem makes reference to the Anastenaria, a fire-walking ritual practiced in several villages in northern Greece and Bulgaria.

"Monolithos": The poets Jack Gilbert and Linda Gregg lived and wrote in the village of Monolithos on Santorini in the late 1960s.

"Morning Sea": This poem responds to a Cavafy poem by the same name.

"Notes for the Invasion": Re'im 10/7/23; Nuseirat, Gaza 6/8/24.

"January Swim": In memory of Adam Zagajewski (1945–2021).

"Days of 1993": The italicized line is from Cavafy, "In the Evening," translated by Edmund Keeley and Philip Sherrard.

"Rembetika Theology": Rembetika celebrates life on the margins of Greek society: hash-smoker's music exiled from Asia Minor to the slums of urban Greece in the 1920s.

"Turning Fifty at the Oracle of Death": The "ancient instructions" (paraphrased in italics) are found in Apuleius, *The Golden Ass* (trans. Robert Graves): "Go there at once and ask to be directed to Taenarus, which is rather an out-of-the-way place to find. It's on a peninsula to the south."

"Gorgona": "Gorgona" is the Greek word for mermaid. In ancient myth, the gorgona was a figure of dread: serpentine and deadly (the most famous gorgona was Medusa). In modern Greek folklore of the northeastern Aegean, these piscine women are figures of aquatic power, equally beloved and feared. The poems in this triptych are spoken by a gorgona on the island of Thasos.

"Nocturne": The poem is in conversation with a poem by Osip Mandelstam, the title of which is sometimes translated as "In the yard at night . . ."

"Days of 2015": The epigraph was written by Michalis Bourboulis, lyrics sung most famously by Sotiria Bellou as "Μην κλαις."

www.ingramcontent.com/pod-product-compliance
Lightning Source LLC
Chambersburg PA
CBHW021652271125
36038CB00002B/63

* 9 7 8 0 8 0 7 1 8 4 7 5 2 *